WHO BUILT THAT?

WHO BUILT THAT?
BRIDGES

An Introduction to Ten Great Bridges and Their Designers

Didier Cornille

Translated by Yolanda Stern Broad

Princeton Architectural Press · New York

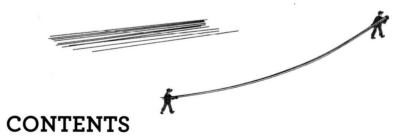

CONTENTS

INTRODUCTION

Since time immemorial, bridges have allowed people to get across obstacles, link cities and villages, and generally get around better. More recently, the development of metal and concrete construction techniques has transformed their design, allowing trains, cars, and trucks to easily cross rivers, streets, and valleys.

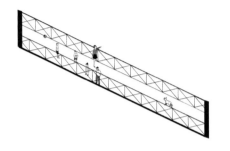

In this book, you will learn about ten fantastic bridges dreamed up by great architects and engineers, the building materials they chose, and the background stories about these often perilous but always fascinating structures.

So come along and have fun as you head into architecture!

1779
IRON BRIDGE

THOMAS FARNOLLS PRITCHARD
THE FIRST CAST-IRON BRIDGE

SPAN: 100 FEET — UNITED KINGDOM

Born in central England, the cradle of the Industrial Revolution,* the British architect Thomas Farnolls Pritchard (1723–1777) first started out as a joiner, following in the footsteps of his father. After establishing his own architectural practice, he went on to build churches and became fascinated with bridges. He studied their structure and sought solutions that were lighter than masonry but longer-lasting than wood.

* The Industrial Revolution was the period from the mid-eighteenth to the mid-nineteenth centuries when new manufacturing technologies drastically changed the way of life in Europe and America.

At the time, European forests were no longer providing enough wood, so people were looking for alternative building materials, such as metal.

In 1735 an iron foundry family, the Darbys, managed to produce the first industrial cast iron, an alloy of iron and carbon. When Pritchard proposed the idea of building a major cast-iron bridge over the Severn River, Abraham Darby III supported him and got the commission to build it. The architect drew the plans for his iron bridge, but, alas, died shortly after construction began. Darby went on to complete the bridge, producing all of the necessary metal pieces in his foundry.

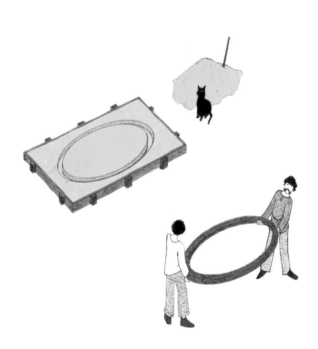

First, workers made a model of each piece of the bridge out of wood. Next, they used the model to make an impression in a bed of sand, into which they then poured the molten iron.

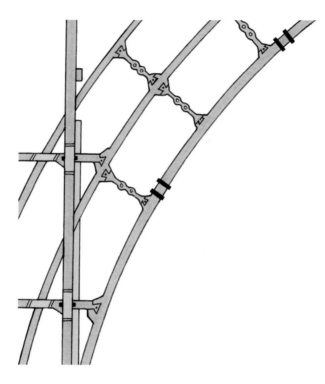

The cast-iron pieces were assembled using carpentry-style metal joints.

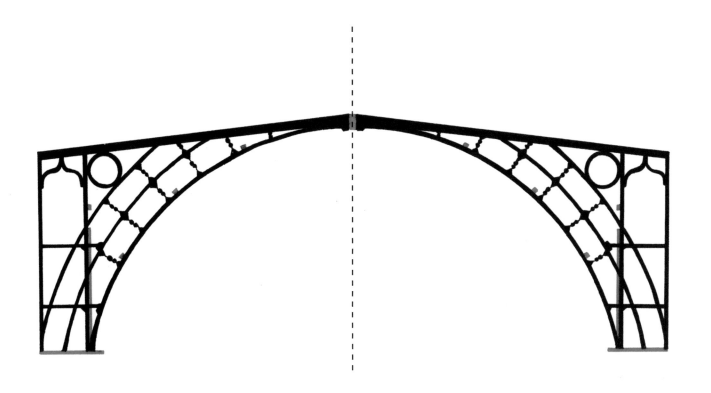

The bridge arch consists of two identical profiles, each 42 ½ feet high.

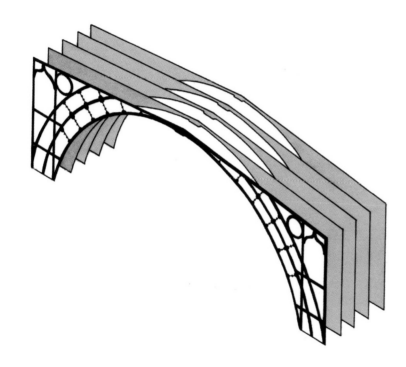

The arch repeats several times to achieve the necessary width of the bridge deck.

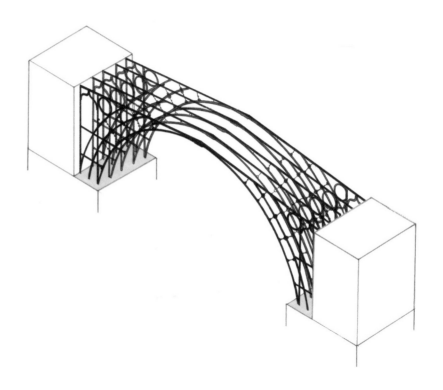

The arches rest on solid masonry supports.

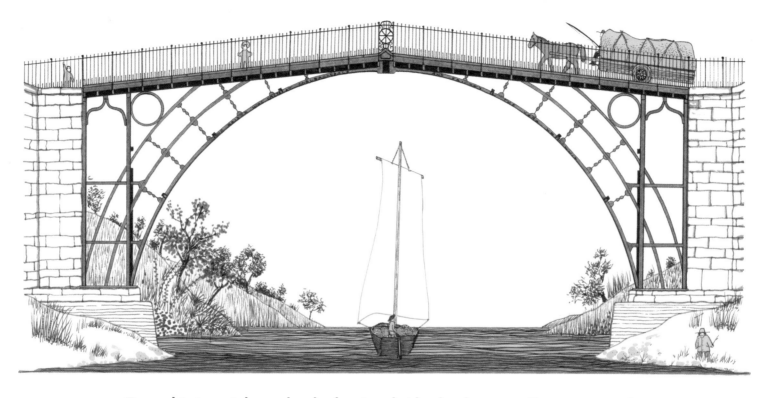

Erected in just eight weeks, the first iron bridge has been used by many travelers.
It is still standing today!

1883
BROOKLYN BRIDGE

JOHN ROEBLING, WASHINGTON ROEBLING & EMILY WARREN

A NEW YORK ADVENTURE

LENGTH: 5,989 FEET — UNITED STATES

German-born engineer John Roebling (1806–1869) immigrated to the United States in 1831, where he became famous for his wire-rope suspension bridges.* After designing the Niagara Falls Suspension Bridge in 1855, he was hired as the chief engineer to design and construct the future Brooklyn Bridge in New York City.

*A suspension bridge is a bridge whose deck hangs from vertical cables that are suspended from master cables running between the bridge's towers.

The idea was to give Brooklynites a way to cross the East River, so they could easily get to work on Manhattan Island; the ferries had long been overloaded. Since the river was a busy waterway, the bridge had to be a tall suspension bridge to allow boats to pass underneath.

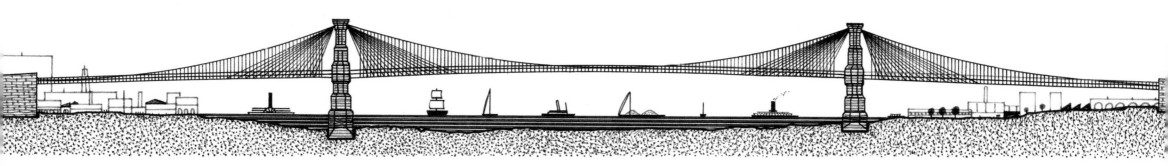

The construction of what was to be the largest bridge ever built at the time started with a tragedy: John Roebling died following an accident involving a ferry that ran into a dock and crushed his foot in 1869. But his son Washington (1837–1926) took over from him, and the work could continue.

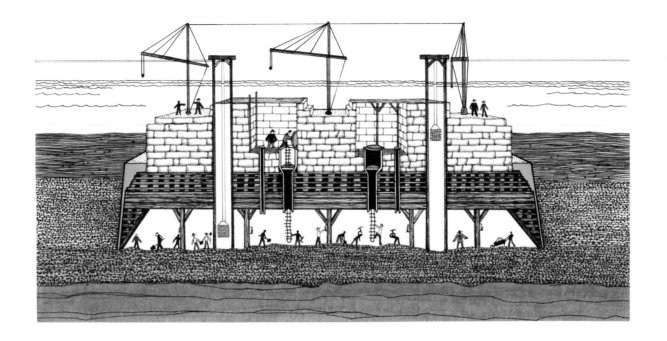

To create the bridge's foundations, Washington Roebling built enormous watertight wooden caissons, resembling large bells, under which the workers could dig up the river bottom. Once they had finished digging, the caissons were filled with concrete and became the piers for the bridge's two towers.

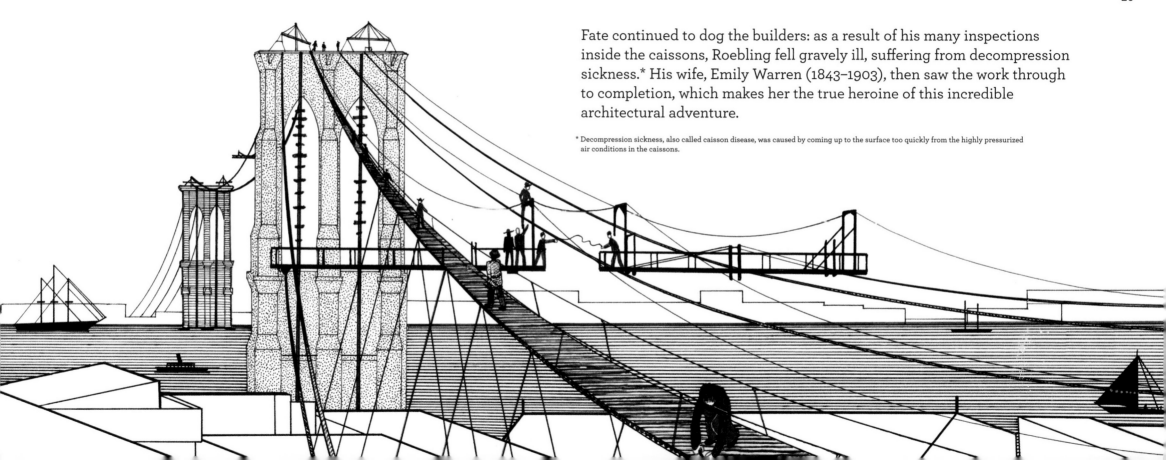

Fate continued to dog the builders: as a result of his many inspections inside the caissons, Roebling fell gravely ill, suffering from decompression sickness.* His wife, Emily Warren (1843–1903), then saw the work through to completion, which makes her the true heroine of this incredible architectural adventure.

* Decompression sickness, also called caisson disease, was caused by coming up to the surface too quickly from the highly pressurized air conditions in the caissons.

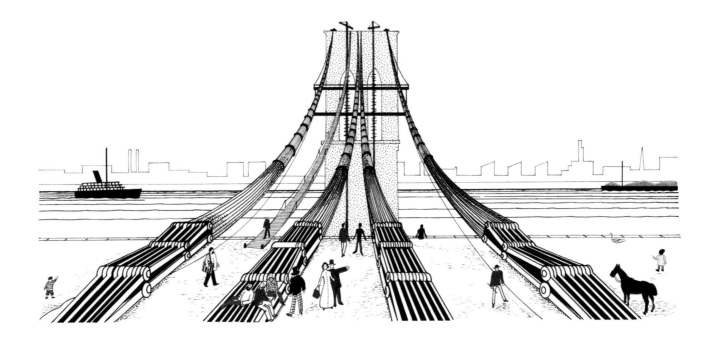

Once the two large towers were erected, steel wires were strung from one riverbank to the other and bound together, forming extra-strong support cables that were anchored to each bank of the river.

The bridge was inaugurated in 1883. A parade of circus animals, including twenty-one elephants, was led across the bridge to demonstrate its sturdiness! Next came pedestrians, trolleys, and all kinds of cars...

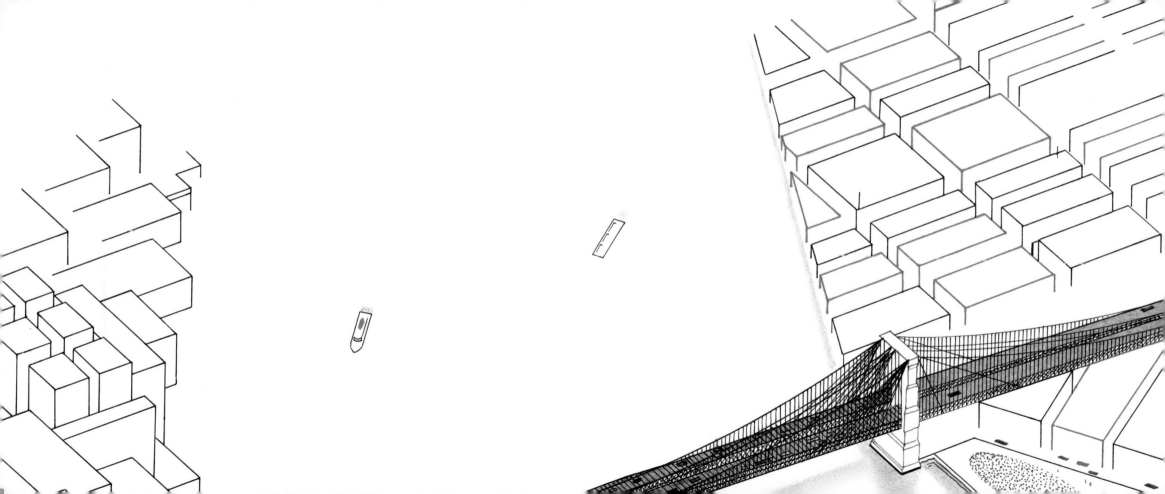

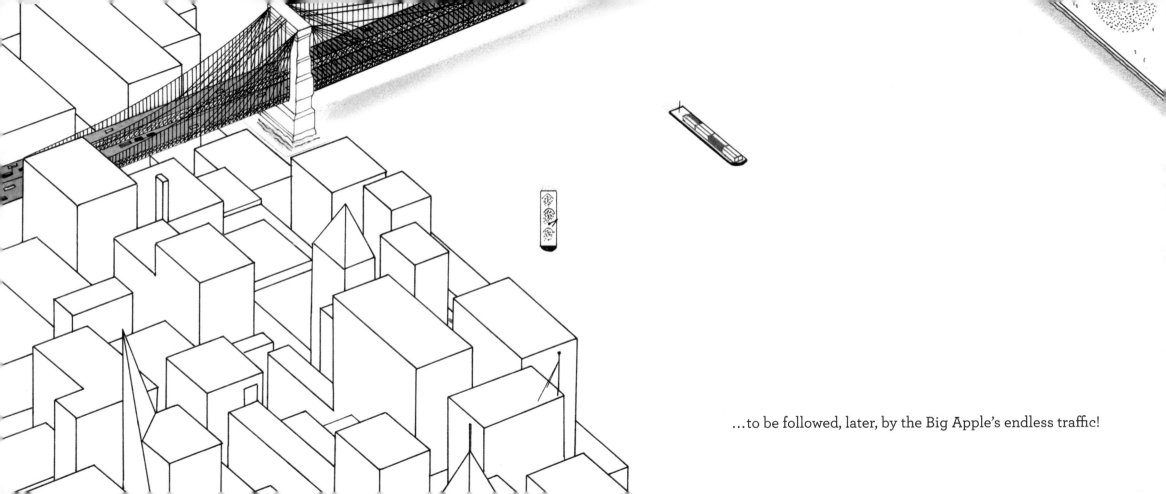

...to be followed, later, by the Big Apple's endless traffic!

1890
FORTH BRIDGE

SIR JOHN FOWLER
& SIR BENJAMIN BAKER
A STEEL DINOSAUR

LENGTH: 8,296 FEET — UNITED KINGDOM

In 1863 John Fowler (1817–1898) and Benjamin Baker (1840–1907), both English engineers, contributed to the construction of the first subway in the world: the London Underground. Fowler also built many railway bridges, and Baker designed a cylindrical boat for transporting an obelisk from Egypt to England, among other engineering feats.

When the British Railway first decided to build a bridge to connect the city of Edinburgh, in southern Scotland, to the Fife region, north of the Forth River estuary, it chose railway engineer Thomas Bouch (1822–1880) as its designer.

But Bouch's excellent reputation was ruined when another structure of his, the bridge over the Tay River, collapsed after a storm in 1879, resulting in many victims.

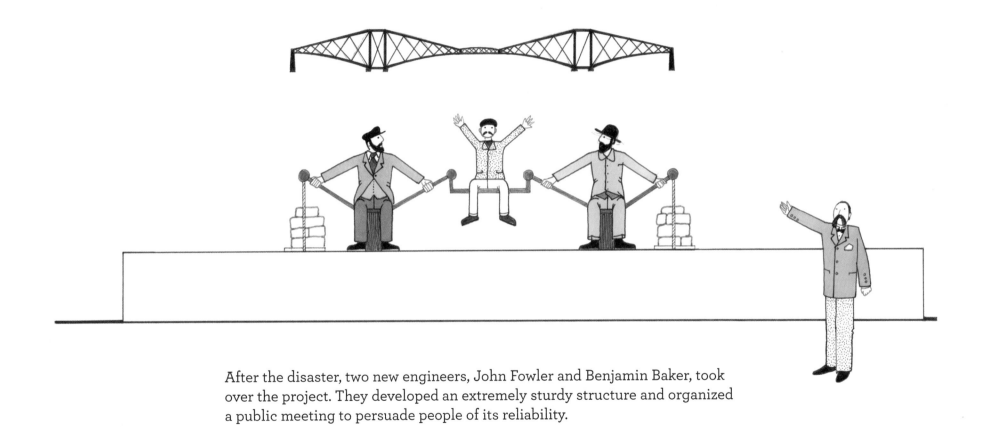

After the disaster, two new engineers, John Fowler and Benjamin Baker, took over the project. They developed an extremely sturdy structure and organized a public meeting to persuade people of its reliability.

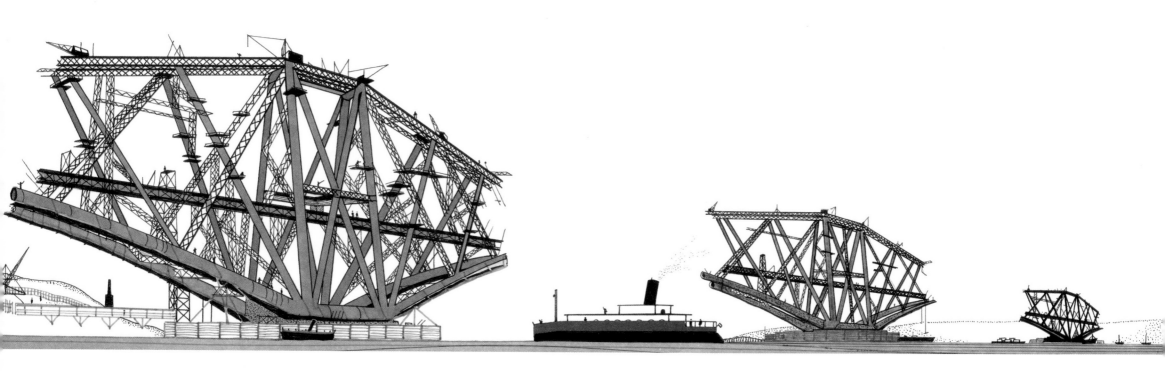

The bridge consists of three diamond-shaped steel cantilever sections, supported by towers that are anchored to the silty river bottom.

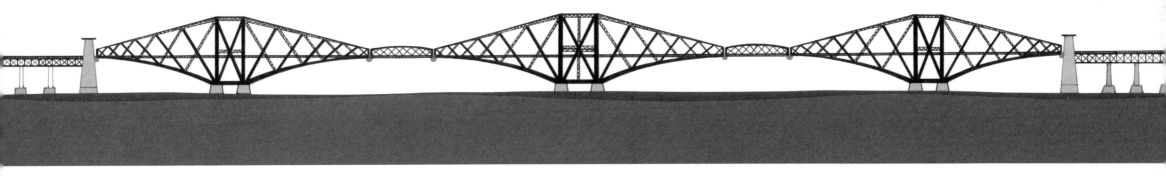

The three sections were then connected to each other by lattice girders.* This meant that the bridge had fewer girders that could collapse.

* A girder is a large beam, usually made of iron or steel.

After the bridge was completed, it was painted red, and the trains started running.

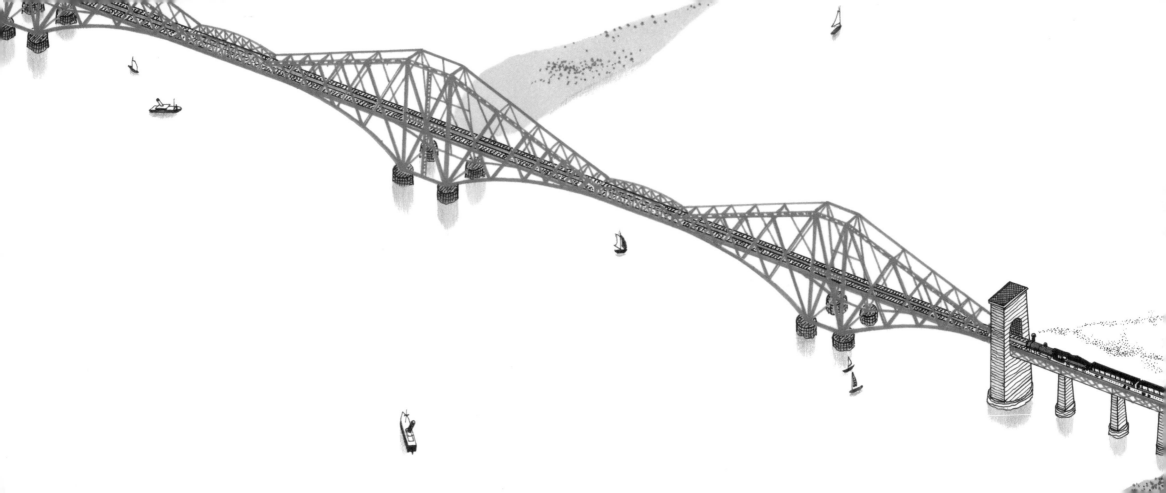

1930
PLOUGASTEL BRIDGE

EUGÈNE FREYSSINET
AN ALL-CONCRETE BRIDGE

LENGTH: 2,913 FEET — FRANCE

Eugène Freyssinet (1879–1962), a French engineer who had graduated from the École polytechnique (Polytechnic Institute) and the École nationale des ponts et chaussées (National School of Bridges and Roadways) in Paris, was fascinated by concrete. As the head of a large construction company, his specialty was building economical, highly innovative bridges.

He invented lightweight reusable timber centering,* which could be moved along a structure as it was built.

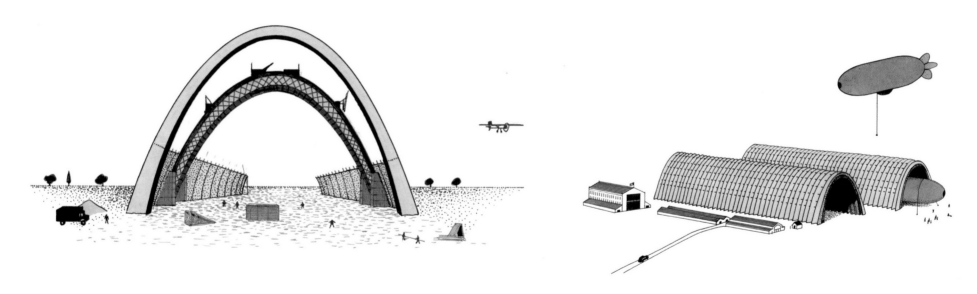

He used it to construct large hangars, like the ones built at the Orly Airport in France (1923) for housing airships.

* Centering is a temporary framework used to support arches and vaults during construction.

The Plougastel Bridge was built to cross the Elorn River between Plougastel-Daoulas and Brest, in western France. Freyssinet won the competition for its design, because his proposal was much less expensive than traditionally constructed steel bridges. He suggested the use of cost-saving reusable centering and many other innovations.

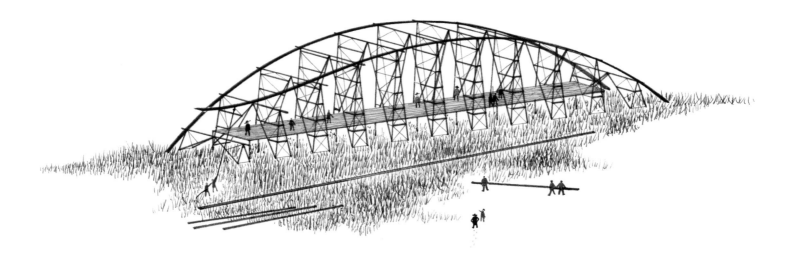

To create the centering for the bridge's arches, long fir boards were first curved on trestles on shore.

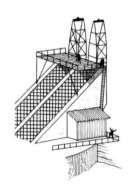
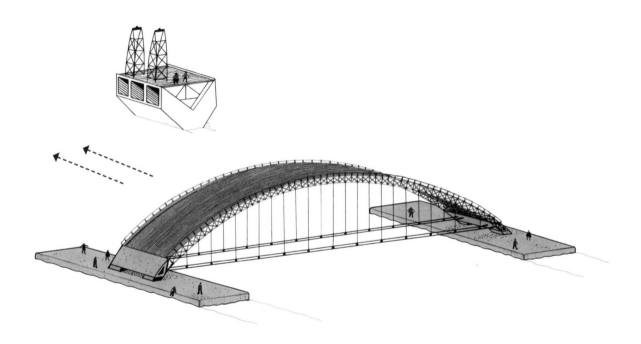

Two concrete barges then hauled the centering across the river to the already installed bridge abutments.

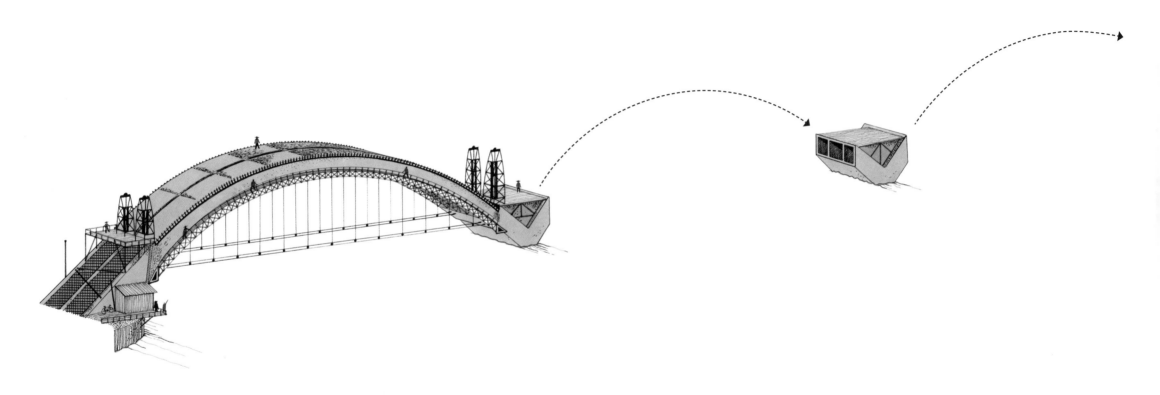

Next concrete was poured for building the first arch. The same centering was then used to build the bridge's other two arches.

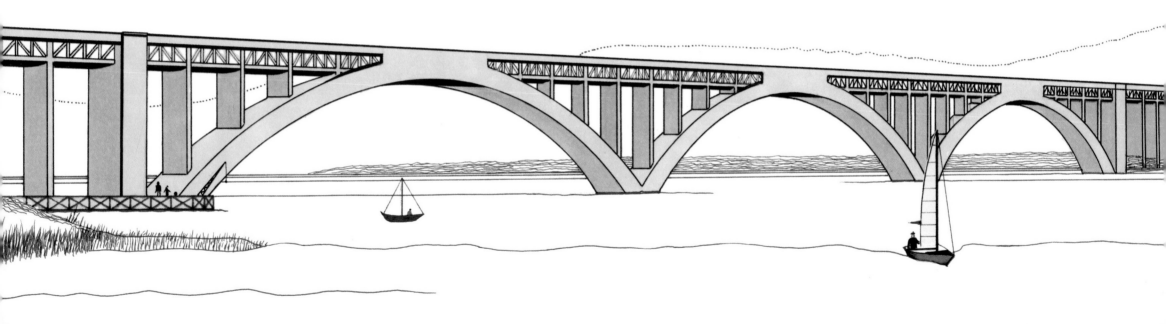

Finally, piers were erected in between the arches to support the bridge's double decks, with a bottom deck for railroad traffic. The Plougastel Bridge, also called the Albert-Louppe Bridge, was finished.

1932
SYDNEY HARBOUR BRIDGE

JOHN JACOB "JOB" CREW BRADFIELD
THE COATHANGER

LENGTH: 3,770 FEET; WIDTH: 160 FEET — AUSTRALIA

John Jacob "Job" Crew Bradfield (1867–1943) was an Australian engineer who specialized in public works and hydraulics, as well as civil engineering and rail transport. He is best known for overseeing the design and construction of the Sydney Harbour Bridge.

The city of Sydney developed on both sides of a magnificent natural harbor during the nineteenth century. People soon decided to build a bridge to make getting across the bay easier. But crossing "the most beautiful harbor in the world" called for an exceptional structure.

After he was appointed to head the project, Bradfield took a trip to the United States and discovered New York City's Hell Gate Bridge, which became his model. Bradfield presented the project design to the engineers of Dorman Long, the British company in charge of building the bridge. It is a single-span steel arch bridge with a suspended deck and two granite pylons to stabilize it.

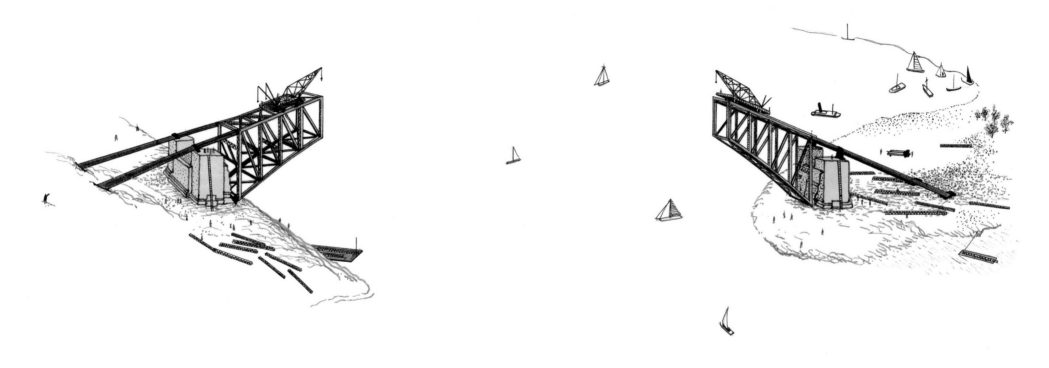

At the start of construction, the two halves of the arch were raised from the abutment towers, with each half held in place by heavy steel cables.

The arch is almost finished. All that remained to do was to slowly loosen the cables until the two sides met.

The finished bridge became the pride of the city and was nicknamed "the Coathanger" by Sydneysiders.

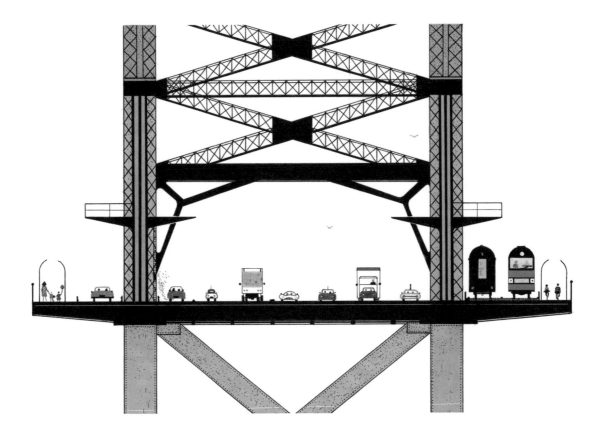

When it was built, it was the widest long-span bridge in the world. You can cross it by car, train, bicycle, or foot: the choice is yours!

1937
GOLDEN GATE BRIDGE

JOSEPH BAERMANN STRAUSS
THE GOLDEN SPAN

LENGTH: 8,980 FEET — UNITED STATES

Joseph Baermann Strauss (1870–1938), an American engineer from Cincinnati, Ohio, started his career at the office of Ralph Modjeski (1861–1940), a pioneer of suspension bridges, in Chicago. After establishing his own firm, Strauss revolutionized the design of drawbridges, but he was always dreaming of achieving even more.

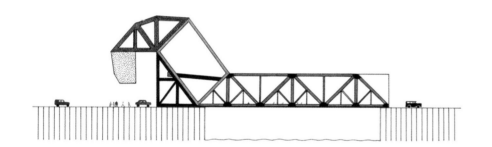
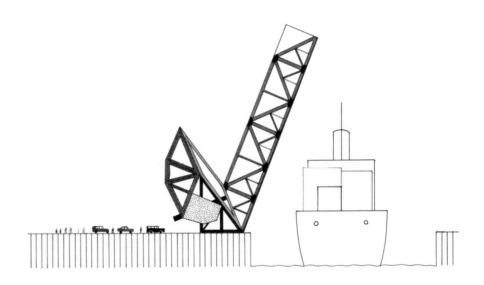

In 1931 he invented the use of concrete counterweights for raising the Cherry Street Strauss Trunnion Bascule Bridge, a drawbridge in Toronto, Canada.

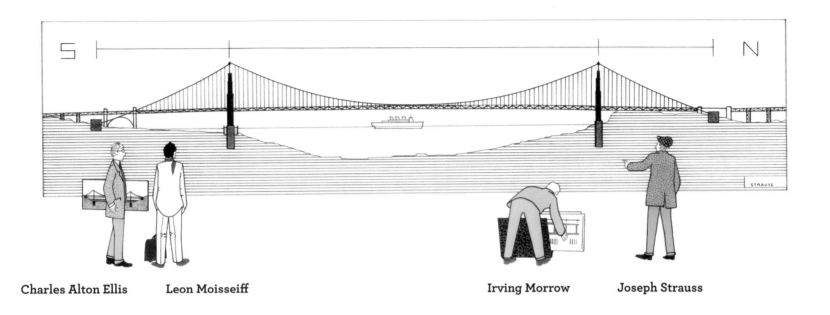

Charles Alton Ellis   Leon Moisseiff   Irving Morrow   Joseph Strauss

But Strauss's most important bridge was a suspension bridge: the Golden Gate Bridge, sponsored by the city of San Francisco and linking it to Marin County, on the other side of the San Francisco Bay. The project was a huge challenge: it meant building the longest and tallest suspension bridge in the world at the time! Strauss pulled together a team of experts to help with the design: Charles Alton Ellis for structural studies; Leon Moisseiff, who created the Manhattan Bridge in New York; and a San Francisco architect, Irving Morrow.

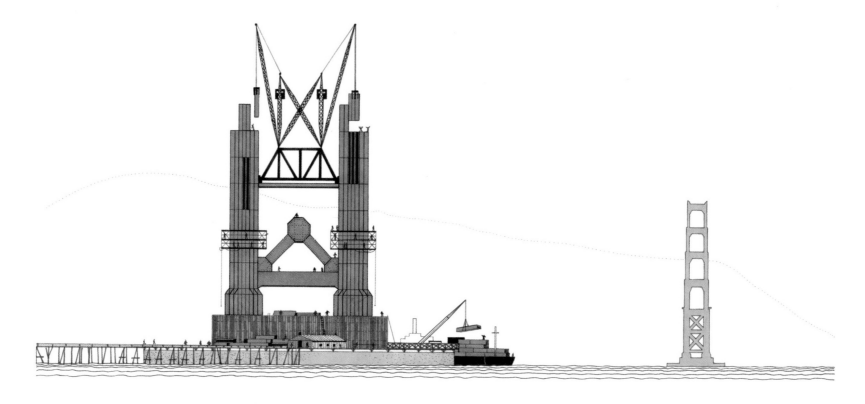

They started by finding a way to deal with the ocean's violent currents, so the bridge's foundations could be dug. Once the foundations were completed, workers raised two huge steel towers skyward.

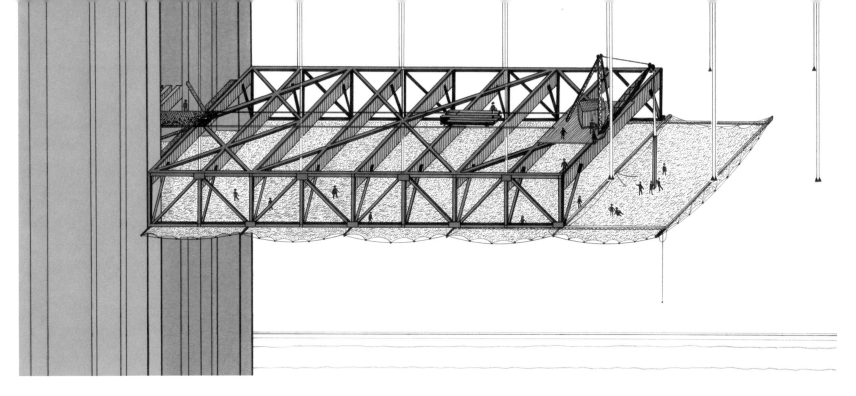

Next the workers assembled the bridge deck. Strauss made sure they stayed safe, making them wear hard hats and installing a huge safety net.

55

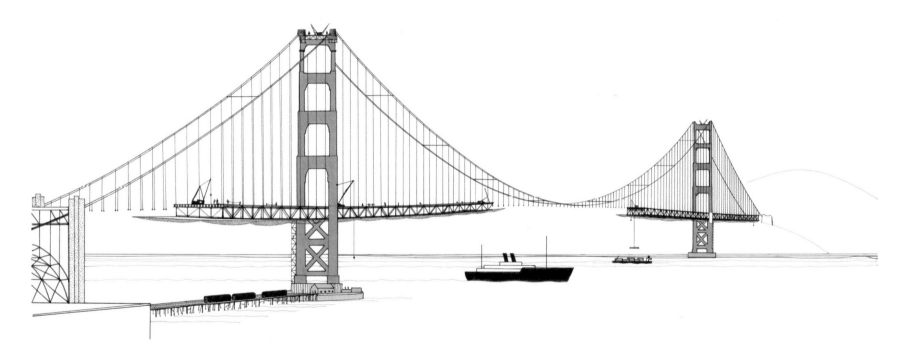

Two enormous main cables were hung from the towers and solidly anchored to the banks on each side of the bay. In addition, 250 vertical cables were installed to support the bridge deck.

Irving Morrow, the architect, chose to paint the bridge a handsome orange color, making it stand out against the ocean and the sky and adding to its beauty.

1974
RIO–NITERÓI BRIDGE

JEAN MULLER
CROSSING THE GUANABARA BAY

LENGTH: 8.25 MILES — BRAZIL

After graduating with a degree in mechanical engineering from the École Centrale Paris (National School of Paris), Jean Muller (1925–2005) started working with Eugène Freyssinet. Later he perfected the method of using precast concrete segments to build large bridges quickly.

The Rio–Niterói Bridge is over eight miles long and links the cities of Rio de Janeiro and Niterói in Brazil. Prefabricating concrete segments is the least expensive option for crossing such great distances.

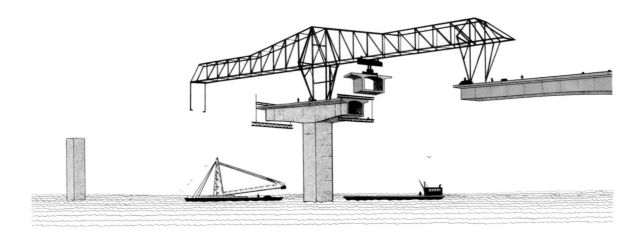

To build the bridge, Muller applied a new construction method, which he first tested when building the Oléron Island bridge in France (1966): a huge steel girder was used as a crane to assemble the precast concrete elements.

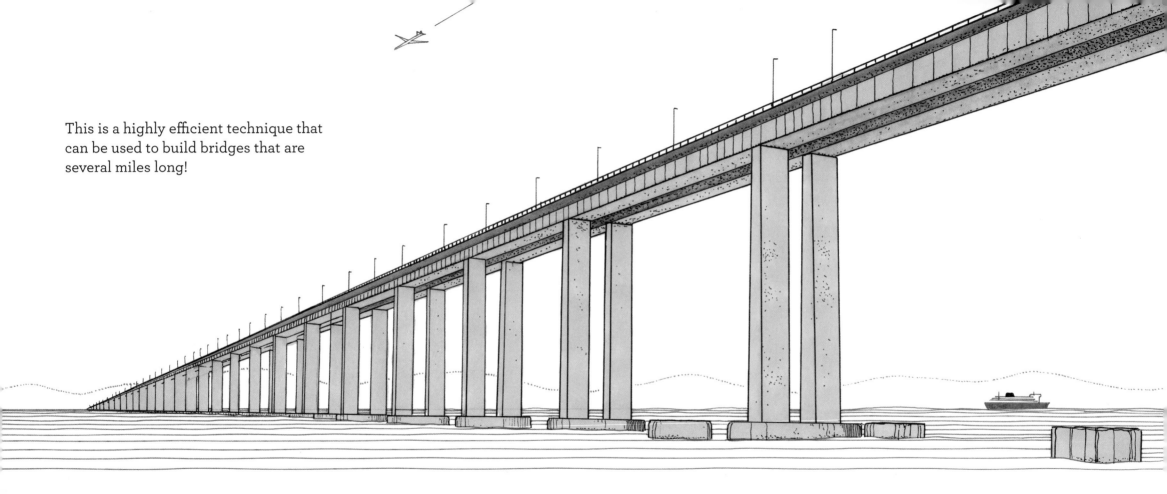

This is a highly efficient technique that can be used to build bridges that are several miles long!

The bridge allows an urban highway to cross Guanabara Bay.

Muller's efficient designs went on to encounter great success, particularly in the United States.

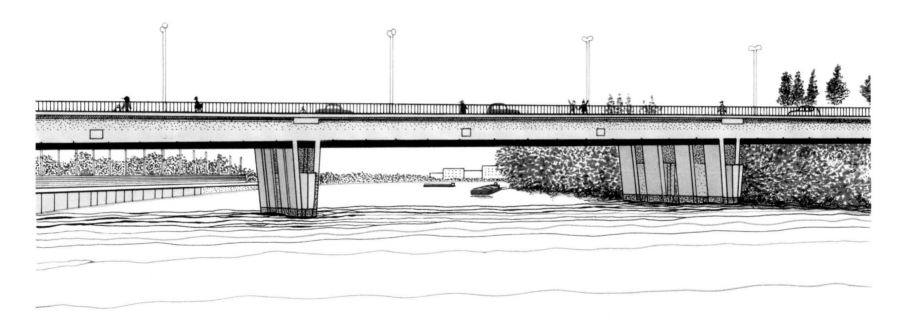

The Choisy-le-Roi Bridge over the Marne River in France (1965) is a simple prefabricated concrete girder.

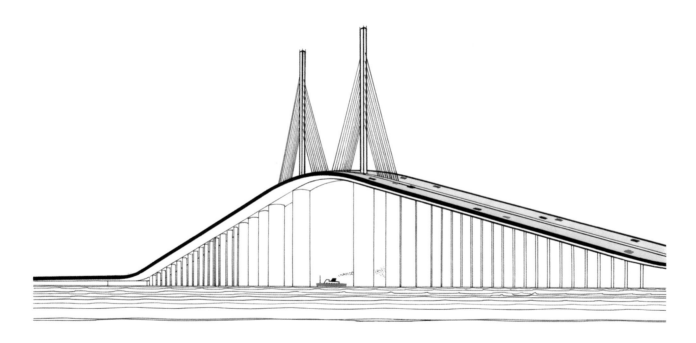

The Sunshine Skyway Bridge across Tampa Bay in Florida (1987)

2004
MILLAU VIADUCT

NORMAN FOSTER & MICHEL VIRLOGEUX
A JOURNEY ACROSS THE SKY

HEIGHT: 885 FEET ABOVE THE TARN RIVER — FRANCE

Norman Foster, born in 1935, is a major British architect. His high-tech buildings combine innovative architecture and integrated design. Michel Virlogeux, born in 1946 and a graduate of the École polytechnique (Polytechnic Institute) and the École nationale des ponts et chaussées (National School of Bridges and Roadways) in Paris, has designed over a hundred bridges.

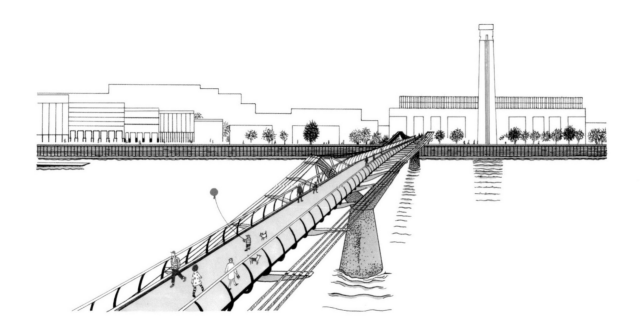

Foster's Millennium Bridge (2000) straddles the Thames River in London and leads to the Tate Modern, a famous art museum.

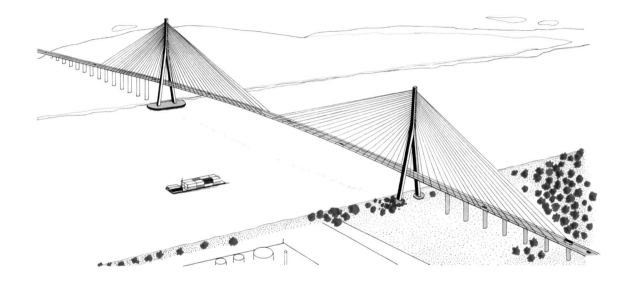

The Normandy Bridge, crossing the Seine River in France, was designed by Virlogeux in 1995.

The Millau Viaduct was built to relieve traffic congestion in the Tarn Valley, through which the Tarn River flows, located on the main route from Paris, France, to Barcelona, Spain. A competition was held, and a number of engineers and architects submitted excellent, inventive solutions.

For instance, the Setec TPI engineering firm, with Francis Soler as the architect, submitted a design with obelisk-shaped piers and steel trusses.

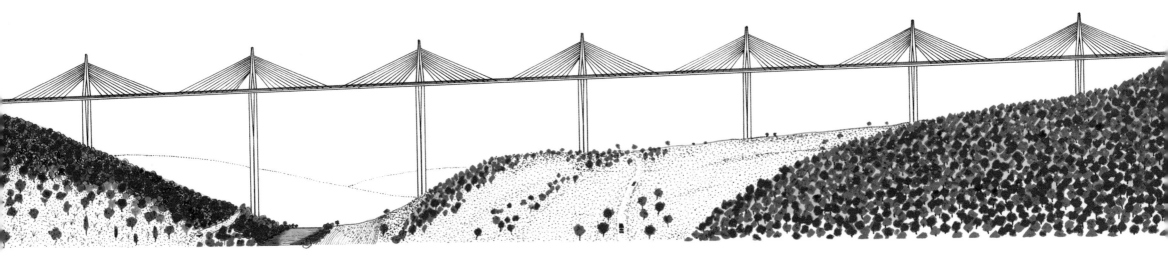

The winning design was submitted jointly by Virlogeux, as the engineer, and Foster, as the architect.
They proposed building a set of seven identical cable-stayed bridges* crossing the whole valley.

* A cable-stayed bridge is a bridge whose deck is supported by cables running to one or more masts.

Construction started, led by the Eiffage Group.
Deep foundations were dug to anchor the piers.

The highest pier, made entirely of reinforced
concrete, is 803 feet tall.

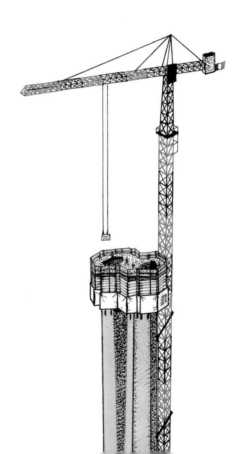

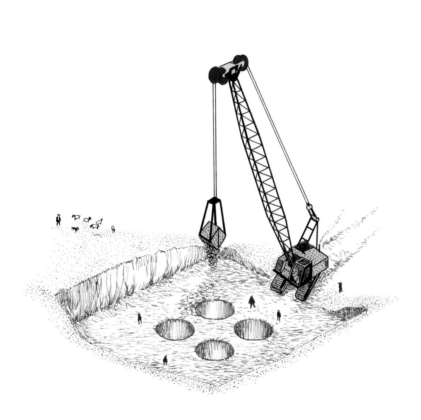

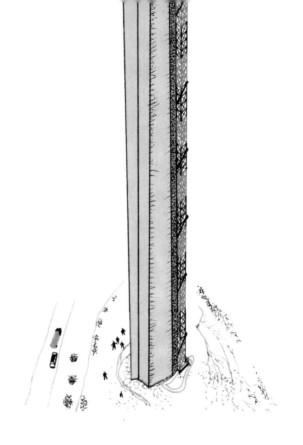

Once the piers were built, temporary supports were raised between them so the bridge deck could be built. Then mast pylons and cable stays were installed.

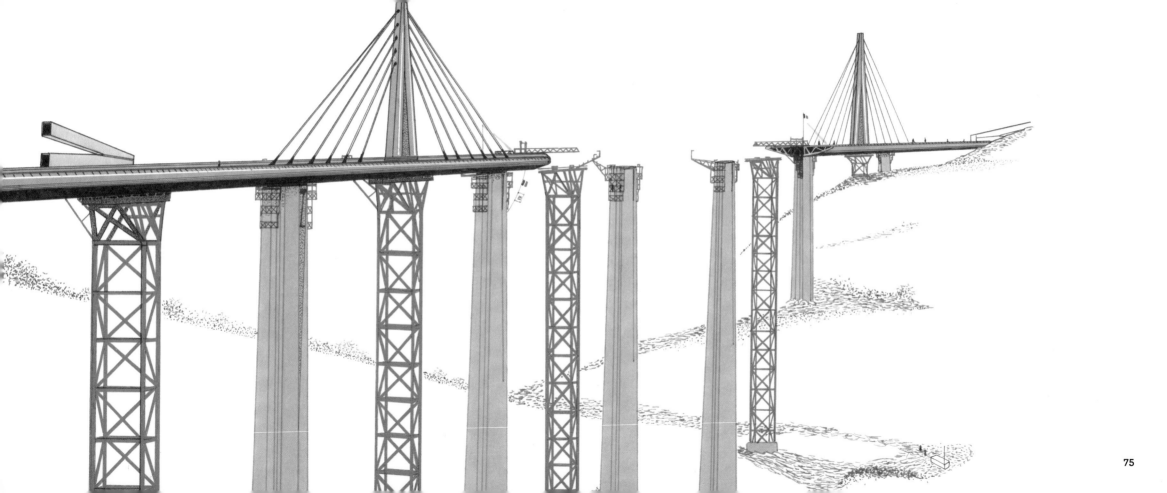

75

The completed bridge is 8,070 feet long, with the tallest pylon measuring 1,125 feet. Its deck crosses the Tarn Valley 885 feet above the river. The Millau Viaduct is not only the highest cable-stayed viaduct in the world, but also an elegant structure that has become a tourist destination.

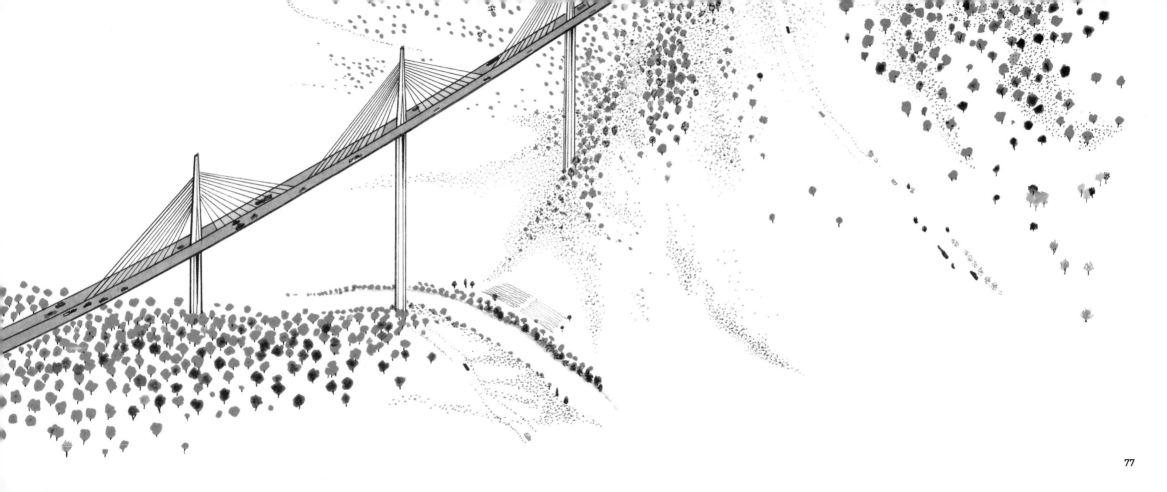

2012
PEACE BRIDGE

SANTIAGO CALATRAVA
A FUTURISTIC WALKWAY SPANNING THE BOW RIVER

LENGTH: 428 FEET — CANADA

Santiago Calatrava, who was born in Valencia, Spain, in 1951, is an artist, architect, and urban planner. He also studied civil engineering, which helps him solve complex technical issues. His creations combine bold forms with highly specialized technology.

The architect has built many bridges, all of which have very interesting shapes that are spectacularly elegant.

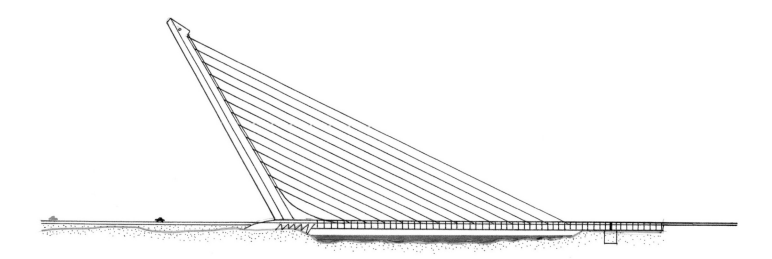

The Alamillo Bridge in Seville, Spain (1992), is a suspension bridge with a single cable-stayed pylon supporting the deck. The entire structure is balanced by the pylon's weight and looks like a giant harp.

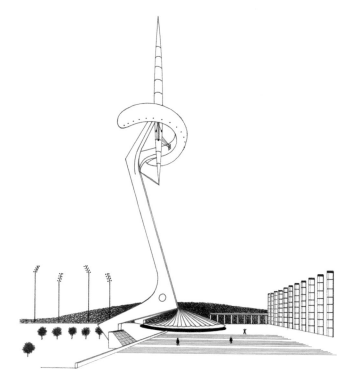

Calatrava also built a number of towers, whose designs often play with the concept of balance. The Montjuïc Communications Tower in Barcelona, Spain (1992), is an excellent example.

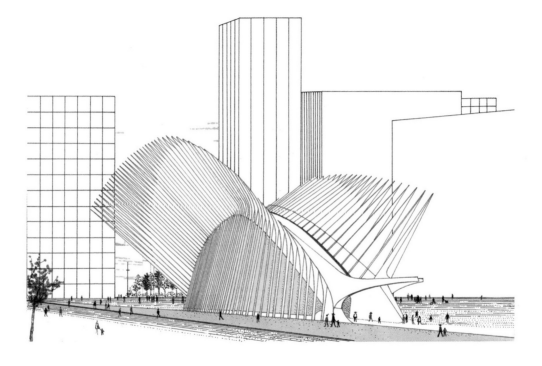

The new World Trade Center Transportation Hub in New York City looks like it is taking flight.
Calatrava's design is a magnificent celebration of the renewal of the southern district of Manhattan.

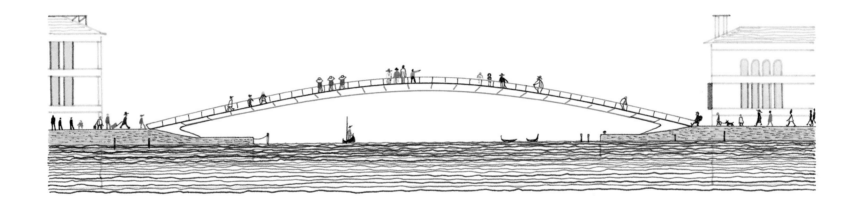

The Constitution Bridge in Venice, Italy (2008), is a contemporary steel structure, but it blends into the city's historic urban landscape discreetly. The delicately vaulted bridge crosses the Grand Canal at the city's entrance.

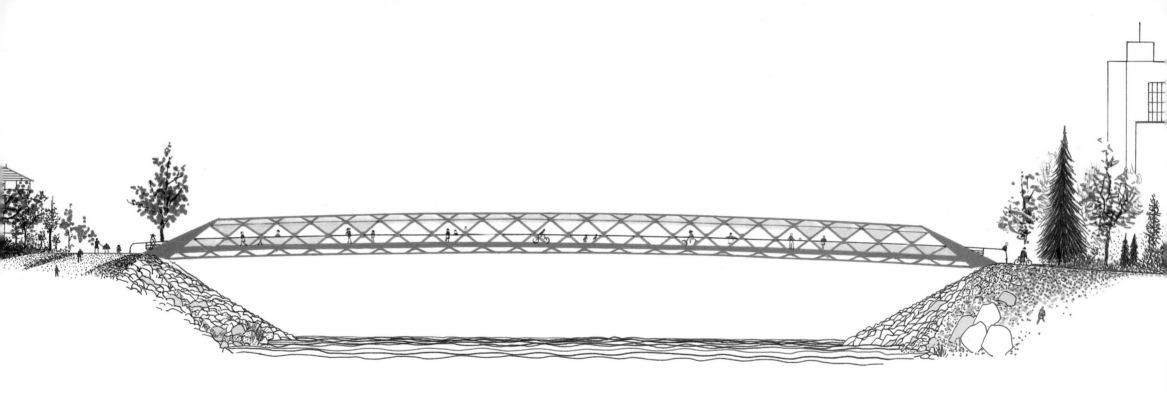

The Peace Bridge in Calgary, Canada (2012), is a footbridge that crosses the Bow River, linking Calgary's downtown to the innercity community of Sunnyside. In order to lessen its impact on the environment, Calatrava designed a bridge without any pillars in the water. He developed an elegant tubular steel structure that rests on both banks of the river and protects people from the city's harsh climate with a glass roof.

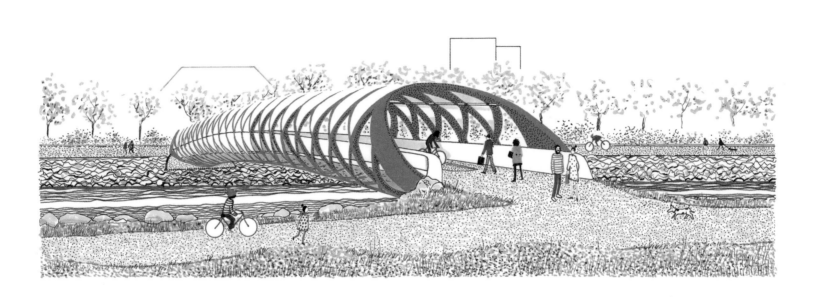

The bridge, which has separate lanes for pedestrians and bicyclists, is painted red and white, the colors of the city and Canada. It is used by up to six thousand people every day.

2013
MUCEM FOOTBRIDGE

RUDY RICCIOTTI
A GENTLE STROLL DOWN TO THE SEA

SPAN: 377 FEET — FRANCE

Born in Algeria in 1952, Rudy Ricciotti later moved to France, where he became an engineer and studied at the École Nationale Supérieure d'Architecture de Marseille (National School of Architecture of Marseille). He is the son of a mason and crazy about concrete. He turned it into a creative material and has received much recognition for his achievements.

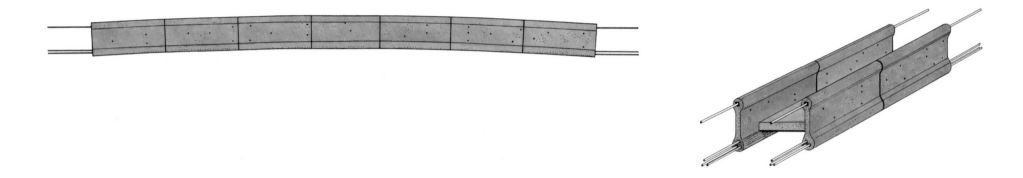

In 2008 Ricciotti built the Passerelle des Anges (Angels' Footbridge) in Gignac, France. With his son Romain, also an engineer, he developed a method for precasting high-performance concrete offsite. Once in place, the prefabricated elements were installed end to end. Then cables were run through them and stretched to form a single large, sturdy girder.

The Angels' Footbridge crosses the Hérault Valley and leads to the Devil's Bridge.

A few years earlier, in 2002, Ricciotti designed the Museum of European and Mediterranean Civilizations (MuCEM), at the entrance to the Old Port of Marseille. He conceived of a large concrete cube surrounded by a latticework shell and planned two walkways linking the museum to the city. The longer one leads visitors to the old Saint-Jean Fort. Completed in 2013, it makes use of the method previously tested in the Angels' Footbridge. The results are astounding.

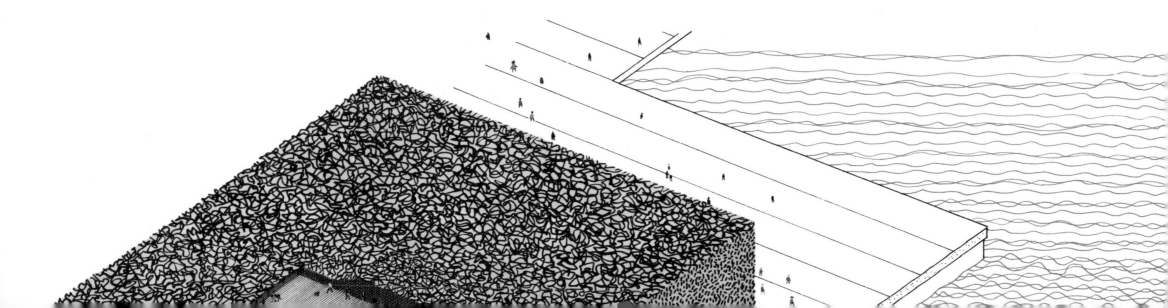

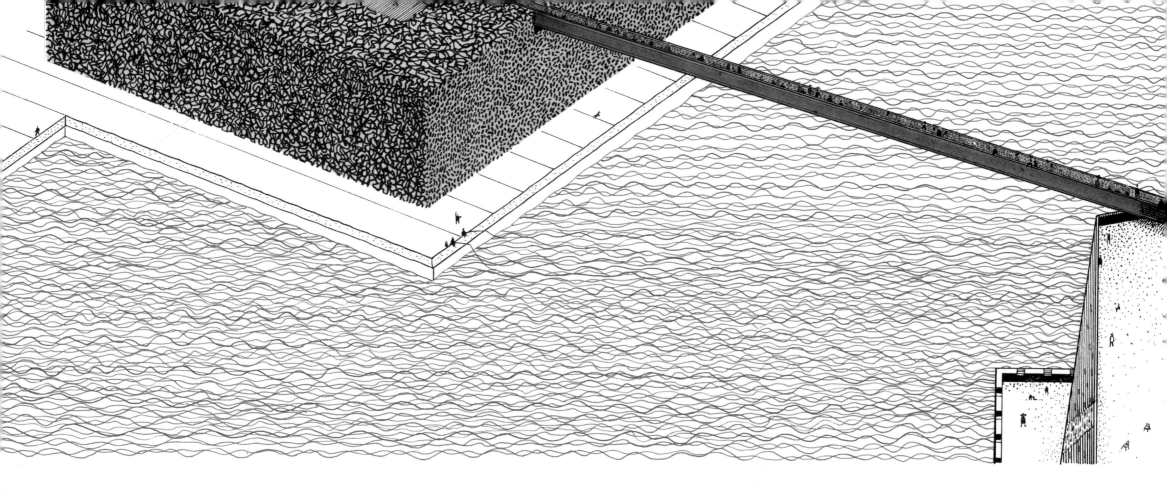

Pedestrian overpasses provide original transit solutions all around the world.

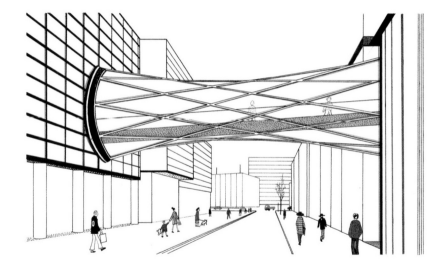

The Corporation Street footbridge by Hodder + Partners in Manchester, United Kingdom (1999), links a department store to the Arndale Centre.

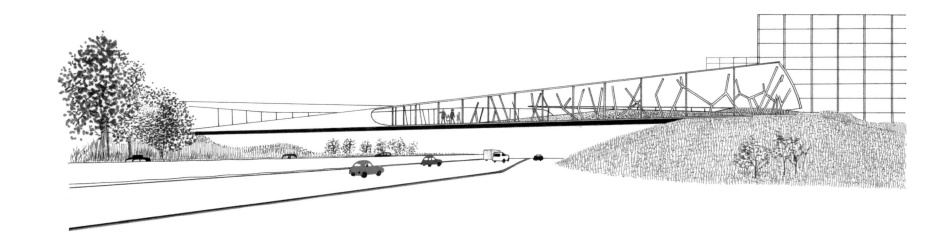

The Landscape footbridge in La Courneuve (France), designed by Marc Mimram in 2008, links the city to a park.

The Valley of the Giants Tree Top Walk near Walpole in western Australia (1957) allows visitors to experience the centuries-old eucalyptus trees while preserving them at the same time.

Published in 2016 by
Princeton Architectural Press
A McEvoy Group company
37 East Seventh Street
New York, New York 10003

Visit our website at www.papress.com

First published in France under the title
Tous les ponts sont dans la nature © 2014
hélium / Actes Sud, Paris, France

English edition
© 2016 Princeton Architectural Press

Designer: Katie Fechtmann

For Princeton Architectural Press
Editor: Nicola Brower
Typesetting: Paul Wagner

Special thanks to: Janet Behning, Abby Bussel, Erin Cain, Tom Cho,
Barbara Darko, Benjamin English, Jenny Florence, Jan Cigliano Hartman,
Lia Hunt, Mia Johnson, Valerie Kamen, Simone Kaplan-Senchak,
Stephanie Leke, Diane Levinson, Jennifer Lippert, Sara McKay,
Jaime Nelson Noven, Rob Shaeffer, Sara Stemen, Joseph Weston, and
Janet Wong of Princeton Architectural Press
—Kevin C. Lippert, publisher

Library of Congress Cataloging-in-Publication Data

Names: Cornille, Didier, 1951- author, illustrator.
Title: Bridges : an introduction to ten great bridges and their architects /
  Didier Cornille ; translated by Yolanda Stern Broad.
Other titles: Tous les ponts sont dans la nature. English
Description: First edition. | New York : Princeton Architectural Press, 2016.
 | Series: Who built that? | First published in France under title: Tous
 les ponts sont dans la nature, c. 2014.
Identifiers: LCCN 2016001407 | ISBN 9781616895167 (hardback)
Subjects: LCSH: Bridges—Juvenile literature. | BISAC: JUVENILE NONFICTION /
 Architecture. | JUVENILE NONFICTION / People & Places / General.
Classification: LCC TG148 .C6713 2016 | DDC 624.2—dc23
LC record available at http://lccn.loc.gov/2016001407w